THE IMPERIAL WAR MUSEUM BOOK OF

WAR BEHIND ENEMY LINES

Julian Thompson joined the Royal Marines a month after his eighteenth birthday and served for thirty-four years, retiring as a Major-General. His service, mainly in the Royal Marine Commandos, took him to seven continents. He commanded 3rd Commando Brigade which carried out the initial landings to repossess the Falkland Islands in 1982, and saw most of the action in the battles that followed.

He is now Visiting Professor in the Department of War Studies, King's College, London. He has presented a series of short Second World War commemorative films on BBC1. As well as writing books on military strategy, the Commando Brigade in the Falklands War and the Parachute Regiment, Julian Thompson also wrote *The Imperial War Museum Book of Victory in Europe* and *The Imperial War Museum Book of the War at Sea*.